APR 1 1

W9-ANH-213

The Little Man In the Map Teaches the

# STATE CAPITALS!

MARYLAND

*MARY'S LAND* HAS APPLE TREES.
MAY I HAVE *AN APPLE, PLEASE?*

ANNAPOLIS

# E. Andrew Martonyi

## Cartoons by Michael Roberts

SP
SCHOOLSIDE PRESS

Woodland Hills, CA

Published by Schoolside Press
www.schoolsidepress.com


Edited by Evelyn Hughes, Present Perfect Writing and Editorial Services
Text and cover design by Mayapriya Long, Bookwrights
Cover illustration by Ed Olson
Cartoon illustrations by Michael Roberts

Printed in the United States of America
11  10  9  8  7  6  5  4  3  2  1

**Publisher's Cataloging-in-Publication**
*(Provided by Quality Books, Inc.)*

Martonyi, E. Andrew (Elod Andrew)
   The little man in the map teaches the state capitals! / by E.
Andrew Martonyi ; illustrations by Michael Roberts. — 1st ed.
    p. cm.
SUMMARY: Teaches the U.S. state capitals by using the memory aids
of word association, rhyme, and cartoon illustrations.
   Audience: Grades 2-12.
   LCCN 2010904804
   ISBN-13: 978-0-9785100-7-7
   ISBN-10: 0-9785100-7-0

   1. Capitals (Cities—United States—Juvenile literature). 2. United
States—Geography—Juvenile literature. [1. Capitals (Cities)—United
States. 2. United States—Geography. 3. Stories in rhyme.] I. Roberts,
Michael, 1964- ill. II. Title.

   G140.M37 2010              917.3
                                        QBI10-600094

Dedicated to my wife
Irma J.
The love of my life

# Acknowledgements

Once again I had the good fortune of working with two very talented editors: Evelyn Hughes of Present Perfect Writing and Editorial Services; and Enikő Gellai, my dear sister, who often disagrees with me but always manages to make the outcome so much better.

Special thanks go to my award-winning art director, Mayapriya Long of Bookwrights, who agreed to take on this project despite her very busy schedule.

I cannot express enough appreciation to Michael Roberts whose clever illustrations enhance the clues. He gave generously of his time and met every challenge with enthusiasm and creativity.

Thanks also to the many students, teachers, and parents who found my first book, *The Little Man In the Map*, a valuable tool for learning the states and encouraged me to use the same concepts for teaching the capitals.

My greatest thanks and admiration go to my wife, Irma, without whose love and support I could not have completed this project.

# Introduction

As a kid growing up, I remember looking at a United States map and thinking how huge the country was and how great it would be to visit all its regions—even all 50 states. At the same time, I found that trying to remember all those states and where they were on the map was very frustrating. Years later, after traveling extensively throughout the U.S. and speaking with many fellow travelers, I learned this was a challenge for many people and an especially difficult one for those who don't travel.

Over the years, I became intrigued with the idea of devising a better way than rote memorization for teaching this information. What technique would make it easy for people to remember each state's name, its shape, and, most important, its location? That challenge led me to write my first book, *The Little Man In the Map: With Clues To Remember All 50 States*. It's a story of fun, imagination, and discovery that helps anyone to learn the states.

The success of that book and its acceptance by teachers, parents, and kids alike—as well as the awards it has received—proved the value of the method it used. Soon I was being urged by students and their parents, by school administrators, and by members of library and teachers' associations to apply my method to other geographic areas of the world. The most frequent request I got, though, was for a new book to teach our state capitals. As it turned out, I had been working on that idea for some time, so I took on the task with great enthusiasm.

For this project, one of my key objectives was to find a straightforward method for readers to link the clue for each capital with the name of its state. A rhyme or catchphrase then highlights the name of the capital, and both elements are reinforced with a humorous cartoon.

Although simple in concept, this venture turned into a lengthy and challenging journey. Nevertheless, the work gave me great satisfaction, and I hope that readers of all ages find as much enjoyment in learning from *The Little Man In the Map Teaches the State Capitals!* as I had in writing it.

E. Andrew Martonyi
Woodland Hills, June 2010

NADA

Lake Superior

MINNESOTA

St Paul

WISCONSIN

Madison

Lake Michigan

MICHIGAN

Lansing

Lake Huron

Lake Ontario

Lake Erie

MAINE

Augusta

Montpelier

VERMONT

NEW HAMPSHIRE

Concord

MASSACHUSETTS

Boston

Providence

Albany

NEW YORK

Hartford

RHODE ISLAND

CONNECTICUT

IOWA

Des Moines

ILLINOIS

Springfield

INDIANA

Indianapolis

OHIO

Columbus

PENNSYLVANIA

Harrisburg

Trenton

NEW JERSEY

Dover

DELAWARE

Annapolis

DC

Washington

MARYLAND

MISSOURI

Jefferson City

Frankfort

WEST VIRGINIA

Charleston

VIRGINIA

Richmond

ATLANTIC OCEAN

KENTUCKY

City

Nashville

TENNESSEE

Raleigh

NORTH CAROLINA

ARKANSAS

Little Rock

Atlanta

Columbia

SOUTH CAROLINA

MISSISSIPPI

ALABAMA

GEORGIA

Jackson

Montgomery

LOUISIANA

Baton Rouge

Tallahassee

FLORIDA

THE BAHAMAS

GULF OF MEXICO

| 0 | 100 | 200 | 300 mi |
| 0 | 100 | 200 | 300 km |

CUBA

# How To Use This Book

In this book, memory aids help you make a connection between a state and its capital that will make it easy to remember that they go together.

To show you how this works, let's have a look at Maryland and all its clues.

*State:* Maryland
*Capital:* Annapolis

*Word Clues:*
Maryland = Mary's land
Annapolis = an apple, please

*Full Clue:*
**Mary's land** *(Maryland)* has apple trees.
May I have **an apple, please** *(Annapolis)*?

• Start by saying the state and its Word Clues (Maryland = Mary's land) and the capital and its Word Clues (Annapolis = an apple, please). Repeat a few times. Listen to the sounds!

## Memory aids make learning easier and a whole lot more fun!

- - - - - - - - - - - - - - - - - - - - - - - - - -

- Next, read the Full Clue that puts the Word Clues of the state and the capital together: **Mary's land** (Maryland) has apple trees. May I have **an apple, please** (Annapolis)?

- Now look at the cartoon to see Mary handing an apple to one of the children. Note how the picture illustrates the full clue.

- Finally, read the easy-to-remember rhyming verse below the picture.

**Mary's land** has apple trees.
May I have **an apple, please**?

That's it! All the clues have worked together to help you remember that Annapolis is the capital of Maryland.

The clues for the rest of the states and their capitals work the same way, with a slight difference for North and South **Carolina** and North and South **Dakota**. For these four states, an additional clue word helps identify which two begin with North and which two with South.

For the **Carolinas**, the added word *needs* emphasizes the letter N in North Carolina, and the word *sound* underscores the letter S in South Carolina.

For the **Dakotas**, the clues include the word *high* for North Dakota, and the word *lower* for South Dakota. (Hold up a map and you'll see that North is always *high*er than South.)

## Have Fun!

# *State:* **Alabama**

## *Word Clues:*

Alabama = Al's pajama

Montgomery = Mount Gummery

## *Full Clue:*

**Al's pajama** *(Alabama)*

on **Mount Gummery** *(Montgomery)*

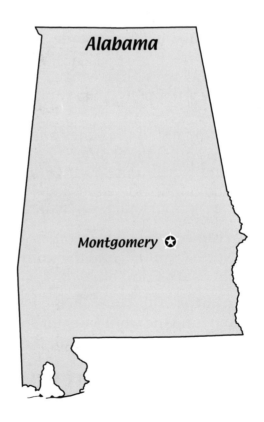

Alabama

Montgomery ✪

## *Capital:* **Montgomery**

*An easy way to remember:*

**Al's pajama**—where can it be?
Look! It's on **Mount Gummery**!

# *State:* **Alaska**

## *Word Clues:*

Alaska = All I ask ya

Juneau = June snow

## *Full Clue:*

**All I ask ya** *(Alaska)*

is for **June snow** *(Juneau).*

# *Capital:* **Juneau**

*An easy way to remember:*

**All I ask ya** and this I pray—
Let **June snow** please come my way.

# *State:* **Arizona**

## *Word Clues:*

Arizona = Arid Zone

Phoenix = fee-nix

## *Full Clue:*

**Arid Zone** *(Arizona)* stall?

**Fee-nix** *(Phoenix)* to fix.

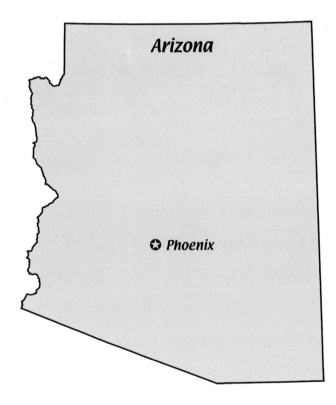

# *Capital:* **Phoenix**

*An easy way to remember:*

**Arid Zone** stall: How much to fix?
What a break! They said, "**Fee-nix**."

# *State:* **Arkansas**

## *Word Clues:*

Arkansas = ark Ann saw

Little Rock = little rock

## *Full Clue:*

The **ark Ann saw** *(Arkansas)*
on the **little rock** *(Little Rock)*

*Arkansas*

✪ *Little Rock*

*Capital:* **Little Rock**

*An easy way to remember:*

Is the **ark Ann saw** upon a dock?
No, it's on a **little rock**.

# *State:* **California**

## *Word Clues:*

California = cauliflower

Sacramento = sack of mementos

## *Full Clue:*

Free **cauliflower** *(California)* with

a **sack of mementos** *(Sacramento)*!

# *Capital:* **Sacramento**

*An easy way to remember:*

Free **cauliflower** with
A **sack of mementos**?
Nobody bought it,
Just held their noses.

# State: **Colorado**

- - -- - -- - -- - -- - -- - -- - -- - -- - --

## Word Clues:

Colorado = collar radio

Denver = den bear

## Full Clue:

The **collar radio** *(Colorado)*

on the **den bear** *(Denver)*

*Colorado*

⭐ *Denver*

*An easy way to remember:*

The **collar radio** made
The **den bear** dance—
"Look at me! No paws or hands!"

# *State:* **Connecticut**

## Word Clues:

Connecticut = connect the cut

Hartford = hardboard

## Full Clue:

**Connect the cut** *(Connecticut)*

**hardboard** *(Hartford).*

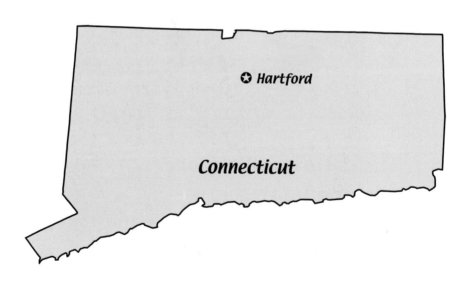

*Capital:* **Hartford**

*An easy way to remember:*

**Connect the cut hardboard**

With patience and glue.
Like learning the capitals—
Easy to do!

# *State:* **Delaware**

## *Word Clues:*

Delaware = Della Wears

Dover = dough-over

## *Full Clue:*

**Della Wears** *(Delaware)*

sells the **dough-over** *(Dover).*

★ Dover

Delaware

# Capital: **Dover**

*An easy way to remember:*

At **Della Wears**, the latest fad?
**Dough-over**—it sells like mad!

*State:* **Florida**

---

## *Word Clues:*

Florida = Flo and Ida

Tallahassee = tall and sassy

## *Full Clue:*

**Flo and Ida** *(Florida)*

are **tall and sassy** *(Tallahassee).*

## *An easy way to remember:*

**Flo and Ida** are **tall and sassy**.
They're the toast of Tallahassee.

# *State:* **Georgia**

## *Word Clues:*

Georgia = George and Gia

Atlanta = at the lantern

## *Full Clue:*

**George and Gia** *(Georgia)* meet
**at the lantern** *(Atlanta).*

# Capital: **Atlanta**

*An easy way to remember:*

**George and Gia** loved at first sight
When they met **at the lantern**'s light.

# State: **Hawaii**

## Word Clues:

Hawaii = how I even

Honolulu = honey Lulu

## Full Clue:

**How I even** (Hawaii) did the hula with my little

**honey Lulu** (Honolulu)

*Hawaii*

*Honolulu*

*An easy way to remember:*

"**How I even** did the hula
With my little **honey Lulu**,"
Was the story he would choose
When people asked about his cruise.

*State:* **Idaho**

## Word Clues:

Idaho = Ida's hoe

Boise = boy, he's noisy

## Full Clue:

**Ida's hoe** *(Idaho)* cut his toe.

**Boy, he's noisy** *(Boise)*!

✪ *Boise*

*Idaho*

# *Capital:* **Boise**

*An easy way to remember:*

**Ida's hoe** cut his toe.
**Boy, he's noisy** in Boise!

*State:* **Illinois**

## Word Clues:

Illinois = ill of noise

Springfield = springs in the field

## Full Clue:

**Ill of noise** *(Illinois)* from

**springs in the field** *(Springfield)*

## *Capital:* **Springfield**

*An easy way to remember:*

He is **ill of noise** from the
**Springs in the field**.
How will his headache
Ever be healed?

# *State:* **Indiana**

## *Word Clues:*

Indiana = Indi and Ana

Indianapolis = Indy nap police

## *Full Clue:*

**Indi and Ana** *(Indiana)*

are the **Indy nap police** *(Indianapolis)*.

Indiana

⊗ *Indianapolis*

# Capital: **Indianapolis**

*An easy way to remember:*

**Indi and Ana** keep the peace.
They are the **Indy nap police**.

*State:* **Iowa**

---

## Word Clues:

Iowa = eye of a

Des Moines = demonstrator

## Full Clue:

**Eye of a** *(Iowa)* gator

on the **demonstrator** *(Des Moines)*

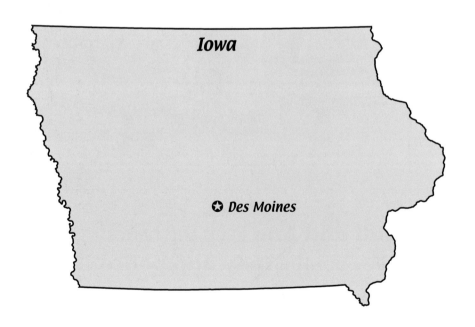

*Iowa*

★ *Des Moines*

# *Capital:* **Des Moines**

*An easy way to remember:*

The **eye of a** gator
Is on the **demonstrator**.

*State:* # Kansas

## Word Clues:

Kansas = can see us

Topeka = to peek a

## Full Clue:

You **can see us** *(Kansas)*,

but you have **to peek a** *(Topeka)* bit.

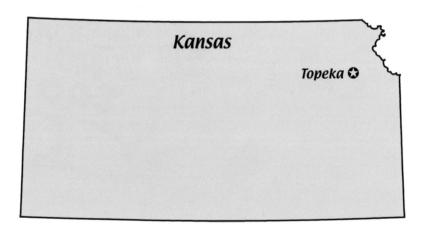

*Capital:* **Topeka**

*An easy way to remember:*

The clowns told the kids,
"You **can see us** dance.
But just **to peek a** bit
Costs 10 cents a glance."

*State:* **Kentucky**

## Word Clues:

Kentucky = Ken took his

Frankfort = franks to the fort

## Full Clue:

**Ken took his** *(Kentucky)*

**franks to the fort** *(Frankfort).*

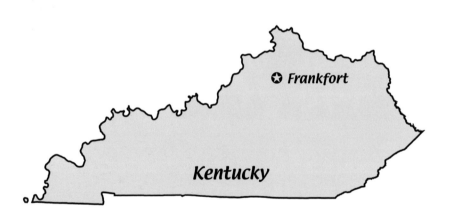

# Capital: **Frankfort**

*An easy way to remember:*

When **Ken took his franks**
**To the fort** each day,
The soldiers there
Would shout, "Hooray!"

*State:* **Louisiana**

## Word Clues:

Louisiana = Louise sees Anna

Baton Rouge = batting for Rouge

## Full Clue:

**Louise sees Anna** *(Louisiana)*

**batting for Rouge** *(Baton Rouge).*

Louisiana

✪ Baton Rouge

*Capital:* **Baton Rouge**

*An easy way to remember:*

When **Louise sees Anna
Batting for Rouge**,
She makes all her pitches
As stingy as Scrooge.

# State: **Maine**

## Word Clues:

Maine = main

Augusta = a gust of

## Full Clue:

The **main** *(Maine)* sail filled
with **a gust of** *(Augusta)* wind.

# *Capital:* **Augusta**

*An easy way to remember:*

As the **main** sail filled
With **a gust of** wind,
The captain was so happy,
He even grinned.

# *State:* **Maryland**

## *Word Clues:*

Maryland = Mary's land

Annapolis = an apple, please

## *Full Clue:*

**Mary's land** *(Maryland)* has apple trees.

May I have **an apple**, **please** *(Annapolis)*?

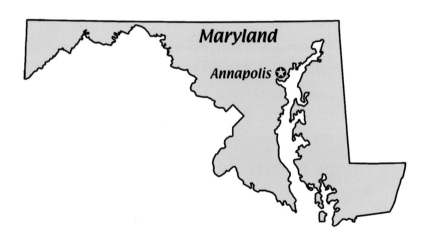

*Capital:* **Annapolis**

*An easy way to remember:*

**Mary's land** has apple trees.
May I have **an apple, please**?

# *State:* **Massachusetts**

## *Word Clues:*

Massachusetts = mass of chewers

Boston = by the ton

## *Full Clue:*

A **mass of chewers** *(Massachusetts)* ate beans

**by the ton** *(Boston).*

# *Capital:* **Boston**

## *An easy way to remember:*

A **mass of chewers** ate and won,
Consuming baked beans **by the ton**.

# *State:* **Michigan**

## *Word Clues:*

Michigan = Mitch began

Lansing = laugh and sing

## *Full Clue:*

**Mitch began** *(Michigan)*

to **laugh and sing** *(Lansing).*

Michigan

Lansing ✪

# *Capital:* **Lansing**

## *An easy way to remember:*

When **Mitch began**
To **laugh and sing**,
The bunny saw a ding-a-ling.

# *State:* **Minnesota**

## *Word Clues:*

Minnesota = mini soda

St. Paul = St. Paul

## *Full Clue:*

**Mini soda** *(Minnesota)* served

by **St. Paul** *(St. Paul)*

St. Paul ✪

*Minnesota*

*Capital:* **St. Paul**

*An easy way to remember:*

The **mini soda** served by **St. Paul**
Is heavenly, but very small.

# *State:* **Mississippi**

## *Word Clues:*

Mississippi = Mrs. Hippy

Jackson = Jack, my son

## *Full Clue:*

"**Mrs. Hippy** *(Mississippi)*,

meet **Jack, my son** *(Jackson)*."

# *Capital:* **Jackson**

*An easy way to remember:*

**Mrs. Hippy** liked to know everyone,
So my mom said,
"Meet **Jack, my son**."

# *State:* **Missouri**

## *Word Clues:*

Missouri = misery

Jefferson City = Jeff's son city

## *Full Clue:*

**Misery** *(Missouri)*, thought

**Jeff's son**. **City** *(Jefferson City)* life for me!

# *Capital:* **Jefferson City**

*An easy way to remember:*

"**Misery** here!" thought **Jeff's son**.
"**City** life would be more fun."

# *State:* **Montana**

## *Word Clues:*

Montana = mountain air

Helena = hail in a

## *Full Clue:*

**Mountain air** *(Montana)* and

**hail in a** *(Helena)* cloud make a bad hair day.

*An easy way to remember:*

She adored the **mountain air**,
But **hail in a** cloud messed up her hair.

# *State:* **Nebraska**

## Word Clues:

Nebraska = new brass cuff

Lincoln = links on

## Full Clue:

His **new brass cuff** *(Nebraska)*

**links on** *(Lincoln)* his sleeve

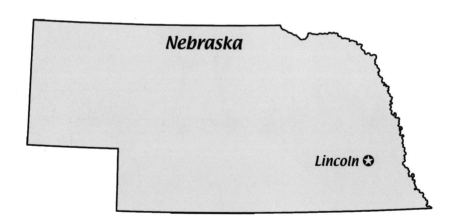

*An easy way to remember:*

On the campaign trail,
Before he could leave,
They saw **new brass cuff
Links on** the president's sleeve.

*State:* **Nevada**

## *Word Clues:*

Nevada = never add a

Carson City = car, son, from the city

## *Full Clue:*

**Never add a** *(Nevada)* **car, son,**

**from the city** *(Carson City).*

*An easy way to remember:*

**Never add a car, son,**
**From the city**,
Or the country car count
Will not be pretty.

# *State:* **New Hampshire**

## *Word Clues:*

New Hampshire = new ham shares

Concord = come on a cord

## *Full Clue:*

The **new ham shares** *(New Hampshire)*

**come on a cord** *(Concord)*.

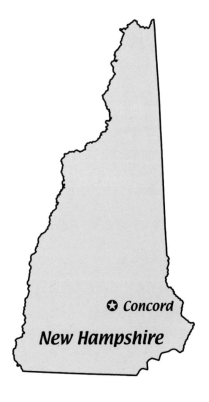

❂ *Concord*

*New Hampshire*

*An easy way to remember:*

The **new ham shares**
That **come on a cord**
We like to play games with
When we are bored.

*State:* **New Jersey**

## *Word Clues:*

New Jersey = new jersey

Trenton = trend on

## *Full Clue:*

His **new jersey** *(New Jersey)*

started a **trend on** *(Trenton)* the beach.

*Capital:* **Trenton**

*An easy way to remember:*

He wore his **new jersey**
On a walk by the bay,
Starting a **trend on**
That very same day.

*State:* **New Mexico**

## *Word Clues:*

New Mexico = new mixers

Santa Fe = Santa's sleigh

## *Full Clue:*

**New mixers** *(New Mexico)* loaded

on **Santa's sleigh** *(Santa Fe)*

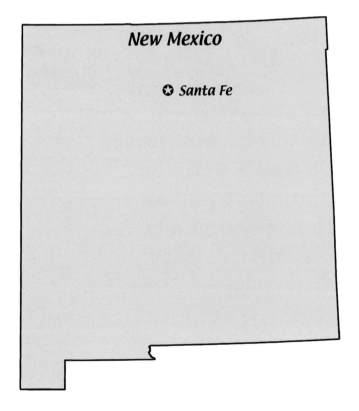

*New Mexico*

✪ *Santa Fe*

# *Capital:* **Santa Fe**

*An easy way to remember:*

**New mixers** got loaded
On **Santa's sleigh**
And blew all the other
Great toys away.

# *State:* **New York**

## *Word Clues:*

New York = New Yorkers

Albany = all baloney

## *Full Clue:*

**New Yorkers** *(New York)* love

**all baloney** *(Albany).*

New York

Albany ✪

# *Capital:* **Albany**

---

## *An easy way to remember:*

**New Yorkers** will always
Stand on line.
To them, **all baloney**
Is just divine.

# *State:* **North Carolina**

(see How To Use This Book, p. 8)

## Word Clues:

North Carolina = North, your caroling needs

Raleigh = rally Lee

## Full Clue:

**North, your caroling n**eeds *(North Carolina)*

to really **rally Lee** *(Raleigh)*!

# *Capital:* **Raleigh**

*An easy way to remember:*

**<u>N</u>orth, your caroling <u>n</u>**eeds
To really **rally Lee**,
But you all sound just like
A timid honeybee.

*State:* **North Dakota**

(see How To Use This Book, p. 8)

## Word Clues:

North Dakota = North Decoders

Bismarck = bee's mark

## Full Clue:

**North Decoders** *(North Dakota)*

scored <u>high</u> as a **bee's mark** *(Bismarck).*

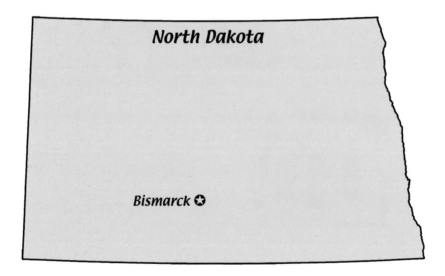

# *Capital:* **Bismarck**

## *An easy way to remember:*

**North Decoders** scored
<u>high</u> as a **bee's mark**,
While South stayed low
As a circling shark.

# *State:* **Ohio**

## *Word Clues:*

Ohio = Oh, hi...oh

Columbus = call a bus

## *Full Clue:*

**Oh**, **hi...oh** *(Ohio)*!

No, **call a bus** *(Columbus)*!

Ohio

Columbus ✪

# *Capital:* **Columbus**

## *An easy way to remember:*

**Oh, hi**...**oh**! No, **call a bus**.
That taxi won't fit all of us.

# *State:* **Oklahoma**

## *Word Clues:*

Oklahoma = OK

Oklahoma City = OK City

## *Full Clue:*

**OK** *(Oklahoma)* has an
**OK City** *(Oklahoma City).*

*An easy way to remember:*

Oklahoma—it's **OK**!
**Just add "City"**
And you're right the whole way.

# *State:* **Oregon**

## *Word Clues:*

Oregon = organ

Salem = sell 'em

## *Full Clue:*

**Organ** *(Oregon)* sale!

Go **sell 'em** *(Salem)*!

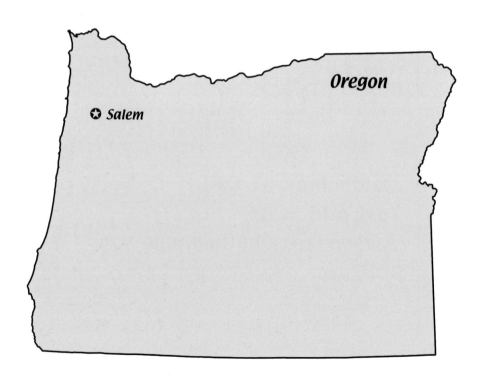

# *Capital:* **Salem**

## *An easy way to remember:*

The **organ** sale has just begun.
**Sell 'em**, guys—let's get it done!

# *State:* **Pennsylvania**

## *Word Clues:*

Pennsylvania = pencil van

Harrisburg = Harry's burgers

## *Full Clue:*

The **pencil van** *(Pennsylvania)* hurried through **Harry's Burgers** *(Harrisburg).*

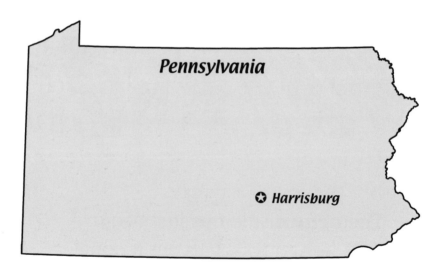

# *Capital:* **Harrisburg**

*An easy way to remember:*

The **pencil van**
Was running late,
But **Harry's Burgers**
Didn't make him wait.

*State:* # Rhode Island

## Word Clues:

Rhode Island = Rhoda, I'll

Providence = prove I dance

## Full Clue:

**Rhoda, I'll** *(Rhode Island)*
**prove I dance** *(Providence).*

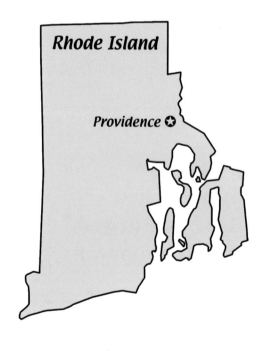

# *Capital:* **Providence**

## *An easy way to remember:*

"**Rhoda**," he pleaded,
"**I'll prove I dance**.
Just give me
Another chance."

*State:* **South Carolina**

(see How To Use This Book, p. 8)

## Word Clues:

South Carolina = South, your caroling sounds

Columbia = column of bees

## Full Clue:

**<u>S</u>outh, your caroling s**ounds *(South Carolina)*

like a **column of bees** *(Columbia).*

*Capital:* **Columbia**

*An easy way to remember:*

**S<u>outh</u>, your caroling <u>s</u>**ounds
Like a **column of bees**—
You're all singing
In different keys.

# *State:* **South Dakota**

(see How To Use This Book, p. 8)

## *Word Clues:*

South Dakota = south decoders

Pierre = pier

## *Full Clue:*

**South Decoders'** *(South Dakota)* scores are <u>lower</u> than a sunken **pier** *(Pierre)*.

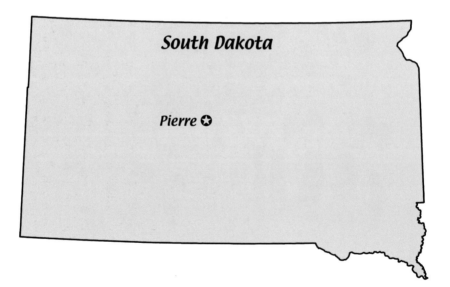

# *Capital:* **Pierre**

## *An easy way to remember:*

**South Decoders'** scores appear
<u>Lower</u> than a sunken **pier**.

*State:* # Tennessee

---

## Word Clues:

Tennessee = "Ten at Sea"

Nashville = gnashing at will

## Full Clue:

The "**Ten at Sea**" *(Tennessee)*

mashed and **gnashed at will** *(Nashville).*

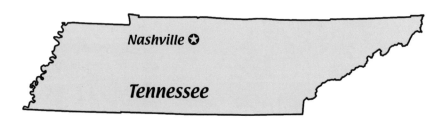

# Capital: **Nashville**

## An easy way to remember:

"**Ten at Sea**" was
Their pirate name.
**Gnashing at will** was
Their favorite game.

# State: **Texas**

## Word Clues:

Texas = Tex-Mex

Austin = awesome

## Full Clue:

**Tex-Mex** *(Texas)* food
is **awesome** *(Austin)*.

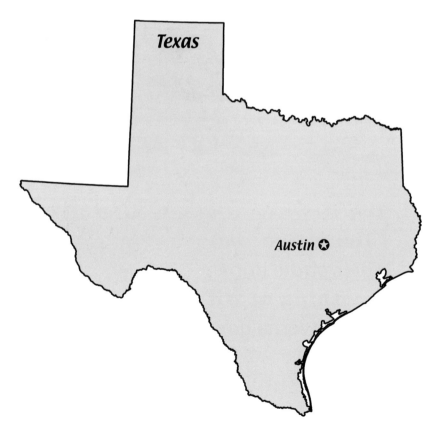

# *Capital:* **Austin**

## *An easy way to remember:*

**Tex-Mex** food is **awesome** to eat.
Everyone says it can't be beat.

## *State:* **Utah**

### *Word Clues:*

Utah = you thaw

Salt Lake City = lake with salt from the city

### *Full Clue:*

**You thaw** *(Utah)* the **lake**

**with salt from the city** *(Salt Lake City)?*

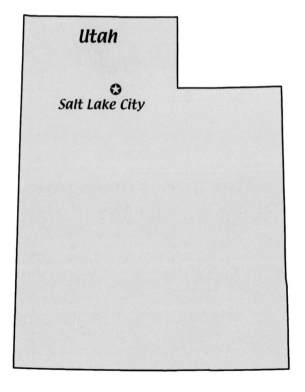

# *Capital:* **Salt Lake City**

## *An easy way to remember:*

**You thaw** the **lake**
**With salt from the city**?
But that salt is
Dirty and gritty!

# *State:* **Vermont**

## *Word Clues:*

Vermont = worm's out

Montpelier = moths beware

## *Full Clue:*

**Worm's out** *(Vermont)*!

**Moths beware** *(Montpelier)*!

## *Capital:* **Montpelier**

*An easy way to remember:*

**Worm's out**! He's loose again!
**Moths beware—**
He'll break his chain.

## *State:* **Virginia**

### *Word Clues:*

Virginia = Virginia

Richmond = rich men

### *Full Clue:*

**Virginia** *(Virginia)* admires

**rich men** *(Richmond)* in vests.

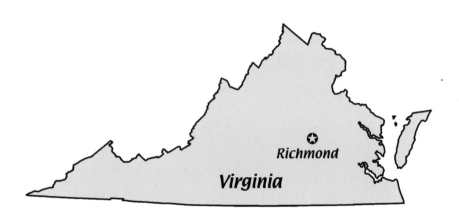

Richmond

*Virginia*

# *Capital:* **Richmond**

*An easy way to remember:*

**Virginia** thinks **rich men** in vests

Are easily the most best dressed.

*State:* **Washington**

## Word Clues:

Washington = washing a ton

Olympia = ole limpy Pa

## Full Clue:

**Washing a ton** *(Washington)*

of clothes for **ole limpy Pa** *(Olympia)*

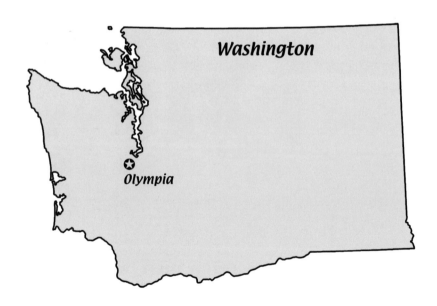

*An easy way to remember:*

**Washing a ton** for **ole limpy Pa**
Was not a task enjoyed by Ma.

# *State:* **West Virginia**

## *Word Clues:*

West Virginia = vest for Virginia

Charleston = Charles charges by the ton

## *Full Clue:*

**Vest for Virginia** *(West Virginia)?*

**Charles charges by the ton** *(Charleston).*

West Virginia

Charleston

*An easy way to remember:*

A **vest for Virginia**?
She wants only one.
But **Charles**
**Charges by the ton**.

# *State:* **Wisconsin**

## Word Clues:

Wisconsin = whisk on some

Madison = medicine

## Full Clue:

**Whisk on some** *(Wisconsin)*

**medicine** *(Madison).*

# *Capital:* **Madison**

*An easy way to remember:*

**"Whisk on some medicine,"**
Is what the bottle said.
"Smack right on the forehead,"
Is what he thought he read.

# State: **Wyoming**

## Word Clues:

Wyoming = Why…oh…me?

Cheyenne = shy Ann

## Full Clue:

"**Why**…**oh**…**me** *(Wyoming)*?"

stammered **shy Ann** *(Cheyenne)*.

Wyoming

Cheyenne ✪

## Capital: **Cheyenne**

An easy way to remember:

"**Why**...**oh**...**me**?"
Stammered **shy Ann**.
"A crown for me?
...You think I can?"

# About the Author

 **E. Andrew Martonyi**'s affinity for travel, his constant search for new things to see, and his granddaughter's fascination with his trips inspired him to study the U.S. map from a new angle. What he discovered he shared in his award-winning book, *The Little Man In the Map: With Clues to Remember All 50 States*, and continues with his newest book that teaches the U.S. capitals.

An author, public speaker, trainer, and businessman, Andrew has toured the world giving seminars to thousands of people. His journeys began early in his youth when his family crossed the Atlantic to land at Ellis Island. As a young man, he drove across the U.S., and the Rocky Mountains, the deserts, and the Pacific Ocean made him fall in love with the West. He lives in California with his wife, Irma, who shares his love of travel and exploration.

# About the Cartoonist

**Michael James Roberts** lives in Adelaide, South Australia. He first drew a comic strip for his local newspaper at age 16. He has been a secondary school teacher for 24 years, with art and cartooning being among the subjects he has taught. He won a statewide cartooning competition with *The Adelaide Advertiser* newspaper in 1996 and has also been a member of the Australian Cartoonists' Association (formerly Black and White Artists' Club).

He has published a single-frame cartoon book, *Inklings*, and illustrated three poetry books for U.S. children's poet Kenn Nesbitt (*My Foot Fell Asleep, I've Seen My Kitchen Sink, Sailing Off To Singapore*).

His passion for cartooning is based on its strong association with humor and the power it has as an effective communicator of ideas by being a form of art that is universally loved by children and adults alike.